D0095818

# MOVING ON FROM THE MIDDLE

## To:

_____

## On Your Graduation From Junior High School

## Date:

_____

## Given to you by:

_____

To my children:

I am always
here for you.

To my parents:

Thanks for doing the
same for me.

A portion of the proceeds
from this book will go to
The Audrey Johnson Theatre
Foundation

Making sure that every
child, regardless of economic
or family situation, is
exposed to live theatre while
growing up.

www.audreyjohnsonfoundation.com

# **INTRODUCTION**
## You
## did it!

You made it through the middle school years.

The years "in between elementary school and high school."

The years in between being a child and being a teenager.

The years in between feeling like you couldn't imagine a world away from your parents and feeling like you can't wait for the next part of your life to begin.

Now, it's on to high school.

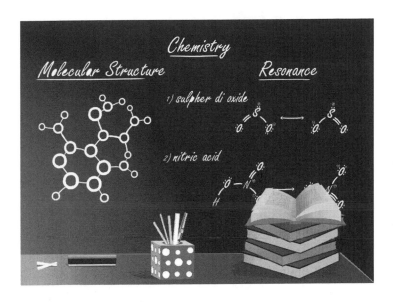

The next four years of your life will be an adventure. As with any adventure, I want you to be ready.

High school is a time for firsts.

First time you will drive a car.

First part-time job.

First time you will go to a "home game."

First homecoming.

First prom.

First love.

First heartbreak.

It's all ahead of you. You are so lucky.

You are probably nervous. You might be scared.

Don't worry.

No matter how confident they look, everyone around you feels the exact same way.

# EVERYONE IS WONDERING

Wondering where they fit in or whom they should befriend.

Wondering how to talk, how to walk and how to act.

Wondering what to wear.

Wondering what's cool and what's not.

Wondering what's "in" and what's "out."

There are no easy answers to any of these questions because the answers always change.

But some things never change.

Before you head off to high school, there are some things that you need to know.

Things that will help you through these next four years.

Things that I wish that someone had told me when I was going into high school.

Your parents grew up in a different era than you did.

The technology has advanced. The kids are different. But high school will always be the same.

CLOTHING STYLES WILL CHANGE.

HAIRSTYLES WILL CHANGE.

THE MUSIC WILL CHANGE.

THE WORLD CHANGES EACH AND EVERY DAY.

BUT THIS ADVICE WILL NEVER GO OUT OF STYLE.

# ONE

# POPULARITY ONLY MATTERS DURING HIGH SCHOOL.

Don't disregard anyone because they aren't cool. They might not be cool right now, but it's very possible they will be one day.

It may seem like everyone has more self-confidence than you do, but I can guarantee that everyone is insecure. No one really knows where they fit in.

Popularity is only an illusion created by others who want you to believe it.

Choose your friends based on how they treat you and make you feel, not on how they affect your social status.

A true friend is there for you when things are bad just as much as they are there when things are good. Ask yourself if the people you have chosen to be friends will both cheer you up and cheer you on.

# THE MOST UNPOPULAR KIDS USUALLY END UP AS THE MOST SUCCESSFUL ONES IN REAL LIFE.

# TWO

## DO NOT GET INTO A CAR WITH A DISTRACTED DRIVER.

A distracted driver is..

A driver who has been drinking.

A driver who is on drugs.

A driver who is texting or playing on the internet or taking a selfie or uploading a picture to Instagram.

That ride can cost you your entire future.  It's not worth it.

Let's come up with a "safe word."  It can be any word that we decide in private. You can use the word on the phone or text it to me when you are feeling uncomfortable in situation.

I will come get you.  No questions asked.

# YOU KNOW THOSE AMAZING THINGS THAT YOU WANT TO DO WHEN YOU GROW UP?

# DON'T LET THEM END BECAUSE YOU WERE TOO EMBARRASSED TO SAY NO TO A RIDE.

# PLEASE!!!

# THREE

# GRADES DO MATTER. BUT PEOPLE-SKILLS WILL ULTIMATELY TRUMP THE HIGHEST HIGH SCHOOL G.P.A.

We want you to work hard in high school.

We want you to challenge yourself. We want you to do your very best.

We want you to understand that your G.P.A <u>does</u> matter when you are applying to colleges or for jobs.

But there is much more to you than a grade point average.

The heads of corporations and presidents of companies are the ones that people can talk to.

They are the guys and girls that can solve problems and create solutions.

They are the ones who can get along with everyone.

No matter how many hours that you study, no matter how many advanced courses that you take, they don't offer the one thing that everyone needs to know: how to become a leader.

Remember to take your head out of your studies and connect with your peers.

# IN YOUR QUEST TO BECOME A NUMBER, DON'T FORGET TO LEARN HOW TO BE A PERSON.

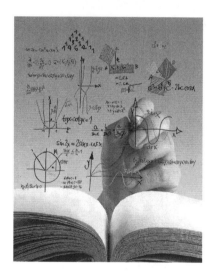

# FOUR

# BAD REPUTATIONS CAN LAST A LIFETIME.

Do not put anything on social media that you don't want to see again in ten years.

When your parents went to high school, we didn't have the internet.  So, silly mistakes that we made in high school only exist in other people's memories today.

But that is not the case for you guys.

Every inappropriate picture, thought, statement, or situation that you find yourself a part of will exist on the Internet forever.

# THINK
# BEFORE YOU
# POST.

## AND PLEASE BE SAFE
## WITH THE FRIENDS
## YOU MAKE ONLINE.
## DANGEROUS PEOPLE
## CAN HIDE BEHIND
## THE INTERNET.

## FIVE

## GET A JOB

Right now, you are living at home with your parents.

Hopefully, you are not worried about paying the rent or where your next meal is coming from.

Unlike college, high school is usually free of charge.

You have free room and board. You get free books and supplies.

But it won't always be this way for you.

# LEARN THE VALUE OF A DOLLAR.

# IT DOESN'T GO AS FAR AS YOU THINK IT DOES.

## SIX

## BE NICE TO EVERYONE. THERE IS NO REASON FOR ANYONE TO BE YOUR ENEMY. YOU NEVER KNOW WHO YOU WILL END UP NEEDING ONE DAY.

The best part of social media is that we are all more connected than ever. You can leave high school knowing that you will always have an idea of what your classmates are doing throughout the rest of their lives.

The people you knew growing up will always have your back. Experiencing high school together is a bond that can never be broken.

The guy you sat next to in science class in 11th grade could be the one in charge of hiring at your dream job.

The girl that you passed in the hall could become a talent agent who gets you the role of a lifetime.

PLEASE DON'T BE
CRUEL TO ANYONE.

PLEASE DON'T BULLY
ANYONE.

PLEASE DON'T BELIEVE
THAT YOU ARE BETTER
THAN ANYONE ELSE.

## A NOTE ABOUT GOSSIP:

Remember the game "Telephone" that you played as a kid?

Everyone sat in a circle. The first person whispered a story to the second person. The story got passed on until the circle ended. That last person would repeat out loud what was whispered to him.

Almost always, it was completely different from the first story.

Gossip is exactly like that. Everyone hears a different version of the same story.

Don't repeat a story to the next person until you know it's got all the right facts.

Just like "Telephone," when you repeat gossip, someone always loses.

# 7.

# EMBRACE IT ALL

Go to the dances. Go to the assembly. Attend the games. Cheer on your team.

These are the memories that last a lifetime: the innocent, silly things you did in high school.

Don't miss a moment.

Laugh a lot.

Hang out with people that you didn't know in middle school.

Sit with new people at lunch whenever you can.

Make friends with all types of kids. Everyone has a story. Many will surprise you. Some will amaze you.

# NOW IS THE TIME TO CREATE MEMORIES:

# YOU WON'T REMEMBER THE TIMES YOU DIDN'T GO.

# YOU WON'T REMEMBER THE FRIENDS YOU DIDN'T MAKE.

## EIGHT

# DON'T BE AFRAID TO TALK TO YOUR PARENTS ABOUT ANYTHING. THERE IS NOTHING THAT YOU ARE GOING THROUGH THAT THEY DIDN'T EXPERIENCE GROWING UP. THEY ARE HERE TO HELP.

We didn't grow up in your world and you didn't grow up in ours. But there is no experience or feeling or emotion you are going through that we aren't aware of.

We will not judge you as long as you are being safe.

We will always love you.

We will not judge you.

We can't help you if you don't tell us what's wrong.

If you don't want to talk to your parents, Please find someone who will listen.

# BUT PLEASE REMEMBER THIS:

# EVERY SINGLE PROBLEM IS TEMPORARY.  IT IS ONLY A MOMENT IN TIME. IT WILL PASS.

# HOW YOU DEAL WITH IT, THOUGH, WILL SHAPE WHO YOU ARE FOREVER.

# NINE

# WHEN YOU EXPERIMENT WITH THINGS THAT CAN HURT YOU, PLEASE BE SAFE.

It is completely unreasonable to think that teenagers are not going to try a sip of alcohol before they are 21. It's naive to think that a teenager won't be tempted through peer pressure or through their own curiosity to try drugs or experiment with sex.

I'm not going to lecture you on why you shouldn't do these things. Because I know the odds are that sometime, in the next four years, you probably will.

If you are going to experiment with alcohol, drugs, or even sex, please do these things in a safe place, with people you trust.

Make good choices for yourself and don't put others in danger.

WE HOPE YOU WAIT UNTIL YOU ARE OLD ENOUGH. WE WISH YOU WOULD WAIT UNTIL IT WAS LEGAL.

BUT MOST OF ALL, WE WISH THAT YOU WILL USE YOUR HEAD AND NOT MESS UP YOUR MIND OR PUT YOUR BODY IN A SITUATION THAT IT'S NOT READY FOR.

# TEN

# CONNECT WITH POPULAR CULTURE.

Find one book, one movie, and one song that you can definitely say is your favorite.

No matter who you are in the hierarchy of the school's social status, when everyone is excited about the latest episode of a new T.V. show or psyched to see that weekend's movie, everyone can relate.

Read the current books that everyone is reading, get into the music that everyone likes, and try out that new reality show that has everyone buzzing.

The one thing that binds teenagers the most is their love of popular culture. Get in on it. Be a part of it. It's the easiest after-school activity there is.

As you get older, those movies that you and your friends loved as a kid, the music that you all listened to, and the books that you read will bring you right back to your youth the minute you see them again.

# YOU WILL ALWAYS REMEMBER WHERE YOU WERE WHEN YOU FIRST SAW YOUR FAVORITE MOVIE, WHO YOU SAW IT WITH, AND HOW IT MADE YOU FEEL.

# ELEVEN

# FIND YOUR VOICE. STAND UP FOR THINGS YOU BELIEVE IN.

Watch the news.

Read the newspaper.

Figure out what matters to you.

You are going to be our next generation of leaders and policymakers.

It will be up to you to decide what your generation stands for.

Speak up if you see something wrong.

Figure out what makes you angry.

Once you do, don't ever let that fire go.

## TWELVE

# DON'T SUBSTITUTE SOCIAL MEDIA FOR HUMAN INTERACTION.

The number of "followers" you have on Instagram or Twitter does not equal the number of real, true friends that you have.

# THE NUMBER OF "LIKES" YOU HAVE ON SOCIAL MEDIA DOES NOT DEFINE HOW MANY PEOPLE LIKE YOU.

## THIRTEEN

# FIGURE OUT WHO YOU ARE NOW. THAT WAY, NO ONE WILL EVER BE ABLE TO TELL YOU WHO YOU SHOULD BE.

Join a club.

Try out for a play.

Take a part-time job.

Take classes in subjects about which you know nothing.

One day soon, the world is going to want you to decide who you are.

There is no better way to do this than to figure out what you enjoy and what you don't.

# FOURTEEN

## HOLD HANDS IN THE HALL.

Not everyone has a high school relationship. But if you do, embrace it.

Being young and in love is a feeling like no other.

Try to keep tokens of your relationships so that when you are older and need a reminder of what young love felt like, you will always remember.

Write love notes.
Keep the ones that are
given to you.

Breaking up hurts, but it
will happen.  It's not the
end of the world.

As you get older, you will
love again.  You will love
harder and deeper.

**RIGHT NOW YOUR JOB IS TO FIGURE OUT WHO YOU ARE AS A WHOLE PERSON BEFORE YOU GIVE HALF OF YOURSELF TO SOMEONE ELSE.**

## FIFTEEN

# LEARN HOW TO LOSE

In real life, not everyone gets a trophy.

Sometimes you succeed and sometimes you fail. Life holds no guarantees of either.

Learn how it feels to win and how it feels to lose.

Learn how to do both with honor.

When you don't win, go over and shake the hand of the person that did.

When you do win, please be humble.

Don't spend too much time patting yourself on the back that you forget that there are others out there who have yet to succeed.

# SIXTEEN

# FIND ONE TEACHER WHO INSPIRES YOU

There are no better role models for you in this world than teachers.

They do not teach for the money or the glory or the fame. (Sadly, none of that comes with teaching.)

They get paid much, much less than professional athletes, movie stars, and famous singers.

They work just as hard as doctors, lawyers, and businessmen.

Find a teacher that you respect. Choose one from whom you learned the most. When you graduate, always stay in touch with that teacher.

The teacher will want to know how you are. You will want to know how that teacher is doing.

And you will want to thank that teacher one day for all that they did for you.

TEACHERS ARE THERE
BECAUSE THEY LOVE WHAT
THEY DO. THEY WANT TO
MAKE A DIFFERENCE IN THE
LIVES OF OUR CHILDREN.

THEY ARE OUR TRUE
ROCK STARS.

# SEVENTEEN

# DON'T FORGET ABOUT YOUR FAMILY

Your siblings may be older or they may be younger. Your grandparents, aunts, uncles and cousins might annoy you or embarrass you.

They are still your family and no matter what, they will always love you.

There will come a day when you no longer live in the same home as your family. You may even move away to a different city, or even a different state.

It's totally o.k.to want to become independent from your family. We want you to learn how to survive without us.

But please, when you can, try and take advantage of your time together.

YOUR FAMILY WILL ALWAYS BE YOUR VERY FIRST FRIENDS.

PLEASE DON'T FORGET ABOUT YOUR OLDEST FRIENDS WHEN YOU ARE OUT THERE MAKING NEW ONES.

# EIGHTEEN

## TAKE CARE OF YOURSELF

Take a break from your studies and turn off all of your electronic distractions.

Get out and breathe the fresh air.

Take a walk or a run.

Join a gym or take a fitness class.

Stay healthy.

Eat right.

Brush your teeth.

Get as much sleep as you can.

# YOU ARE BECOMING AN ADULT.

# PLEASE TAKE CARE OF YOUR NEW BODY.

# IT'S THE ONLY ONE YOU WILL GET.

(Also:
remember to brush
your hair and put on a
clean shirt.
Appearance really
does matter. )

# NINETEEN

## DON'T RUSH

Slow down.

Relax.

Enjoy.

Stop and look around.

Take it all in.

# DON'T BE SO BUSY RUSHING TO GROW UP OR TRYING TO GET SOMEPLACE NEW THAT YOU DON'T ENJOY THE RIDE THAT TAKES YOU THERE.

# TWENTY

# BE HAPPY

You will learn a lot of things in high school, but if you only learn one lesson these next four years, I hope that it is this:

There is no school in the world that can teach you how to be happy. If there were, I would send you there.

This is up to you. Figure out what makes you happiest and strive to have that in your life every day.

# MORE ADVICE FROM YOUR OWN PARENTS

---

---

---

---

---

---

# MORE ADVICE FROM YOUR OWN PARENTS

_____

_____

_____

_____

_____

_____

# MORE ADVICE FROM YOUR OWN PARENTS

_____

_____

_____

_____

_____

_____

# MORE ADVICE FROM YOUR OWN PARENTS

_____

_____

_____

_____

_____

_____

# Also by
## Allyson Ochs Primack

"You'll Be Swell: What To Expect When You Expect Your Child Will Be A Star"

"Mom On The Road"

Check out her blog at:
www.momontour.com

*I get by with a little help from my friends.*
-The Beatles

Special thanks to all of the amazing friends in my life.

Some of you I have known forever, and some of you I have only known a little while.

No matter when we met, I continue to learn from you and to lean on you.

I need strong, true friendships today just as much as I did when I was high school.

Thanks for being there to cheer me up and to cheer me on.

21553957R00051

Made in the USA
Middletown, DE
03 July 2015